WONDER WOMAN

WONDER WOMAN

VOLUME 7
WAR-TORN

WRITTEN BY
MEREDITH FINCH

PENCILS BY
DAVID FINCH
GORAN SUDŽUKA

INKS BY
RICHARD FRIEND
JONATHAN GLAPION
BATT
DANNY MIKI
SONIA OBACK
GORAN SUDŽUKA
JOHNNY DESJARDINS

COLOR BY
SONIA OBACK
PETER STEIGERWALD
BRAD ANDERSON
IVE SVORCINA

LETTERS BY
SAL CIPRIANO
DEZI SIENTY
ROB LEIGH
TOM NAPOLITANO

COLLECTION COVER ART BY
DAVID FINCH
RICHARD FRIEND
SONIA OBACK

WONDER WOMAN CREATED BY
WILLIAM MOULTON MARSTON

SUPERMAN CREATED BY
JERRY SIEGEL &
JOE SHUSTER
BY SPECIAL ARRANGEMENT
WITH THE JERRY SIEGEL FAMILY

MATT IDELSON MIKE COTTON Editors – Original Series
PAUL KAMINSKI Associate Editor – Original Series
DAVID PIÑA Assistant Editor – Original Series
LIZ ERICKSON Editor
JEB WOODARD Group Editor – Collected Editions
DAMIAN RYLAND Publication Design

BOB HARRAS Senior VP – Editor-in-Chief, DC Comics

DIANE NELSON President
DAN DIDIO and JIM LEE Co-Publishers
GEOFF JOHNS Chief Creative Officer
AMIT DESAI Senior VP – Marketing & Global Franchise Management
NAIRI GARDINER Senior VP – Finance
SAM ADES VP – Digital Marketing
BOBBIE CHASE VP – Talent Development
MARK CHIARELLO Senior VP – Art, Design & Collected Editions
JOHN CUNNINGHAM VP – Content Strategy
ANNE DEPIES VP – Strategy Planning & Reporting
DON FALLETTI VP – Manufacturing Operations
LAWRENCE GANEM VP – Editorial Administration & Talent Relations
ALISON GILL Senior VP – Manufacturing & Operations
HANK KANALZ Senior VP – Editorial Strategy & Administration
JAY KOGAN VP – Legal Affairs
DEREK MADDALENA Senior VP – Sales & Business Development
DAN MIRON VP – Sales Planning & Trade Development
NICK NAPOLITANO VP – Manufacturing Administration
CAROL ROEDER VP – Marketing
EDDIE SCANNELL VP – Mass Account & Digital Sales
SUSAN SHEPPARD VP – Business Affairs
COURTNEY SIMMONS Senior VP – Publicity & Communications
JIM (SKI) SOKOLOWSKI VP – Comic Book Specialty & Newsstand Sales

WONDER WOMAN VOLUME 7: WAR-TORN

Published by DC Comics. Compilation Copyright © 2015 DC Comics. All Rights Reserved.

Originally published in single magazine form in WONDER WOMAN 36-40, WONDER WOMAN ANNUAL 1 © 2014, 2015 DC Comics.
All Rights Reserved. All characters, their distinctive likenesses and related elements featured in this publication are trademarks
of DC Comics. The stories, characters and incidents featured in this publication are entirely fictional. DC Comics does not read
or accept unsolicited ideas, stories or artwork.

DC Comics, 4000 Warner Blvd., Burbank, CA 91522
A Warner Bros. Entertainment Company.
Printed by RR Donnelley, Salem, VA, USA. 7/31/15. First Printing.
ISBN: 978-1-4012-5679-1

Library of Congress Cataloging-in-Publication Data

Finch, Meredith.
Wonder Woman. Vol. 7, War torn / Meredith Finch, writer ; David Finch, Sonia Oback, artists.
pages cm
Collects WONDER WOMAN #36-42"-- Provided by publisher.
ISBN 978-1-4012-5679-1 (hardback)
1. Graphic novels. I. Finch, David, 1972- illustrator. II. Oback, Sonia, illustrator. III. Title. IV. Title: War torn.
PN6728.W6F48 2015
741.5'973--dc23
2015024571

PEFC Certified

Printed on paper from
sustainably managed
forests and controlled
sources

PEFC/29-31-75   www.pefc.org

IT NOURISHES AND SUSTAINS LIFE.

BUT IT CAN ALSO BRING DEVASTATION AND DEATH.

IT IS THE
EVIDENCE OF
OUR SORROW.

OR THE
SOURCE OF
OUR JOY.

IT IS THE
ANSWER TO
A PRAYER.

OR OUR WORST
NIGHTMARE.

I WILL NOT STAND FOR IT.

DIANA HAS ALWAYS ACTED LIKE SHE WAS ABOVE US, AND NOW *THIS?!*

MAYBE SHE'S RIGHT, MAYBE IT IS TIME FOR US TO CHANGE.

HOW CAN THROWING AWAY CENTURIES OF TRADITION BE RIGHT? HOW CAN IGNORING EVERYTHING THAT WE HAVE STOOD FOR BE RIGHT?

I WOULD RATHER DIE THAN LIVE ANOTHER DAY ON AN ISLAND POLLUTED WITH THE STINK OF MAN.

CAN YOU NOT BEND EVEN A LITTLE, CLYEMNE?

YOU KNOW THE NATURE OF MAN AS WELL AS I DO, DESSA.

SHOULD WE BOW OUR HEADS AND ALLOW THEM TO SUBJUGATE US, AS THEY HAVE THE WOMEN OF EARTH FOR MILLENNIA?

HAVE YOU SO *COMPLETELY* LOST TOUCH WITH YOUR HUMANITY?

WHAT IS YOUR PROBLEM?

OOMPH!

FOOM

UGGH.

...IS YOUR PROBLEM.

SPLORCH

ENOUGH!

I'M GOING TO CHOOSE NOT TO TAKE THIS PERSONALLY.

I FELT A MASSIVE DISTURBANCE IN THE GREEN AND CAME TO INVESTIGATE. I'M NOT RESPONSIBLE FOR WHAT'S HAPPENED HERE.

SWAMP THING?

I'M SORRY I CAN'T OFFER MORE INSIGHT, WONDER WOMAN, BUT I'LL LET YOU, OR MY FAVORITE JUSTICE LEAGUER OVER THERE, KNOW IF I FIND ANYTHING.

...SHOULD I LET MYSELF DOWN?

UHHH... WHAT JUST HAPPENED?

YOU'RE LUCKY HOLLAND WAS IN A GOOD MOOD.

CATCHING YOUR ENEMY BY SURPRISE IS BASIC STRATEGY.

TRUE. BUT YOU SHOULD KNOW WHO THE ENEMY IS FIRST.

NOW WE KNOW HE DIDN'T DO IT. LET'S MOVE ON.

WHAT'S GOING ON, DIANA? I'VE NEVER SEEN YOU LIKE THIS BEFORE...SO ANGRY.

REALLY?! IT SURPRISES YOU THAT THE SENSELESS DEATHS OF THOUSANDS OF MEN, WOMEN AND CHILDREN ANGERS ME?

YOU'VE HAD TO MAKE TOO MANY TOUGH CHOICES LATELY...

I APPRECIATE YOUR CONCERN, CLARK...

...BUT I'M FINE. *REALLY.*

YOU AND I BOTH KNOW THAT'S A LIE.

WHAT I KNOW IS THAT I'M TIRED.

LET'S CALL IT A DAY AND HIT THE SHOWERS.

...OUR CHOICES...

...AND OUR SACRIFICES...

AELLA, WATCH YOUR *FLANK!*

CLYEMNE, FOLLOW ME.

BREMUSA, TAKE THE CENTER.

DERINOE, NO!

HRRAGH!

WHAT DO YOU THINK YOU ARE DOING?!

DO I LOOK LIKE ONE OF YOUR *MEWLING* HUMANS IN NEED OF RESCUING?

OF COURSE NOT, I JUST...

WHAT WERE THOSE THINGS?

MAN-EATING *STYMPHALIAN BIRDS*--ARES' IDEA OF PETS. THEY STARTED ATTACKING ABOUT A WEEK AGO.

THEY ARE DRAWN TO THE HOME OF THEIR NEW MASTER. BE GRATEFUL THEY COME HERE AND NOT THE LAND OF MEN. WE, AT LEAST, HAVE THE TOOLS TO DEFEND OURSELVES.

THOSE *THINGS* BELONGED TO ARES? I...I HAD NO IDEA...

ANOTHER RESPONSIBILITY YOU HAVE NEGLECTED. YOUR EXCUSES ARE AS THIN AS YOUR COMMITMENT TO THE AMAZONS.

SO BUSY PLAYING GOD AND HERO, YOU KNOW NOTHING OF WHAT IS HAPPENING TO THE PEOPLE YOU CLAIM TO RULE.

OUR PEOPLE DESERVE BETTER THAN THAT.

THEY DO.

AND IF THE AMAZONS REALLY ARE BEING ATTACKED BY CREATURES THAT ONCE BELONGED TO ARES, IT'S MY RESPONSIBILITY AS GOD OF WAR, AND AS QUEEN, TO MAKE THINGS RIGHT.

DIANA, THIS IS CYBORG.

ANOTHER VILLAGE HAS VANISHED.

WE NEED YOU. NOW!

ANOTHER PROBLEM IN THE WORLD OF MEN?

I'LL BE BACK. I PROMISE.

I'LL DEAL WITH THIS.

WE ALL MAKE CHOICES, GIRL.

BUT I WONDER...

...ARE YOU PREPARED TO LIVE WITH THE CONSEQUENCES OF YOURS?

GET THOSE WOUNDED OUT OF HERE!

FALL BACK! FALL BACK, DAMN IT!

WE'LL COVER YOU AS LONG AS WE CAN!

WHA...?

WHAT *HAPPENED* HERE? WHERE'S *DESSA*?

DO I LOOK LIKE I HAVE TIME TO ANSWER YOUR *QUESTIONS*?

"MAYBE IF YOU'D *BEEN* HERE..."

DESSA-- WHERE *IS* SHE?

THE INJURED ARE TOO NUMEROUS. WE DON'T HAVE TIME TO REMEMBER NAMES.

ANYONE? SPEAK UP. SOMEONE *MUST* HAVE SEEN HER.

SHE'S... ON THE BEACH.

SHE STAYED BEHIND SO THAT WE COULD GET THE WOUNDED OUT.

DESSA! DESSA, WHERE ARE YOU?!

NO!

WHAT HAPPENED HERE?

...DRAGON...

...WASN'T STRONG ENOUGH... NEEDED YOU...

WHY DIDN'T YOU CO...

OH, DESSA... I'M SO SORRY...

IT'S TOO DARK DOWN THERE. TURN ON YOUR LIGHTS SO WE CAN SEE.

SORRY ABOUT THAT.

HEY, I'M GETTING A LOT OF BUZZING THROUGH MY COM.

WHOA--!

CLARK! WHAT'S GOING ON DOWN THERE?

CLARK?!

CLARK!

I STAND BEFORE THIS COUNCIL AND ASK--*WHERE* IS OUR QUEEN?

THE BATTLE AGAINST HER WINGED BEASTS IS BARELY WON, AND SHE HAS *ALREADY* ABANDONED US.

YOU *KNOW* SHE IS FIGHTING WITH THE JUSTICE LEAGUE.

DIANA'S RESPONSIBILITIES ARE BIGGER THAN JUST THEMYSCIRA.

AND WHAT OF HER RESPONSIBILITY TO THE AMAZONS?

WHAT IS IMPORTANT IS THAT SHE WAS HERE WHEN SHE WAS NEEDED.

WE WILL WAIT NO LONGER.

DIANA'S ABSENCE HERE TODAY TELLS US THAT SHE HAS *MADE* HER CHOICE.

NOW IS THE TIME FOR US TO MAKE *OURS*.

DERINOE. BRING FORTH YOUR PERFECT AMAZON, THAT WE MIGHT JUDGE HER WORTHINESS FOR OURSELVES.

SHOW US THIS WARRIOR MAIDEN.

SISTERS, YOU KNOW I HAVE PRAYED TO HERA FOR SALVATION.

THAT SHE ONCE *AGAIN* LOOK WITH FAVOR UPON US, FORGIVE US THE SINS OF OUR QUEEN, AND BLESS US WITH A *NEW* CHAMPION.

I PRESENT TO YOU AN AMAZON MAIDEN--A *TRUE* DAUGHTER OF NO MAN--THE ULTIMATE WARRIOR--A QUEEN *WORTHY* OF THE AMAZON NATION.

I MISS YOU SO MUCH.

I WASN'T WRONG TODAY... WAS I?

AM I REALLY SO DIFFERENT NOW?

THAT DEPENDS ON WHOM YOU ASK.

RELATIONS WITH THE CAPITAL HAVE GROWN INCREASINGLY HOSTILE, AND THEN, TWO DAYS AGO, THEMYSCIRA CLOSED ITS GATES TO US.

AFTER THE BATTLE WITH THE FIRST BORN, I THOUGHT WE'D MOVED PAST ALL OF THIS MISTRUST.

THESE WOMEN TRADED US FOR WEAPONS WHEN WE WERE INFANTS. WE WERE FOOLISH TO THINK WE COULD EVER COME BACK.

NISOS, TRUST ME. I KNOW THIS CAN WORK. THEY JUST NEED MORE TIME.

PERHAPS. OR PERHAPS WE'RE ASKING THEM FOR SOMETHING IT'S SIMPLY NOT IN THEM TO GIVE.

I'LL TALK TO THEM. DON'T WORRY. THIS IS GOING TO WORK.

I PROMISE.

BE CAREFUL, DIANA. YOU DON'T KNOW WHAT YOU ARE WALKING INTO.

FEAR.

NONE OF US ARE IMMUNE.

LOOK WHAT IT HAS DONE TO MY SISTERS.

FIGHTING AMONG OURSELVES-- TOO AFRAID TO ACCEPT THE CHANGE OUR BROTHERS REPRESENT.

PROVE YOUR COMMITMENT, DIANA!

PROVE THAT YOU ARE WORTHY TO BE YOUR MOTHER'S HEIR, TO BE CALLED AMAZON-- TO BE *QUEEN.*

SOMEHOW I KNEW IT WOULD COME DOWN TO THIS. FOR ME... IN THIS PLACE... IT ALWAYS DOES.

IS THERE NO OTHER WAY TO END THIS?

IF YOU ARE *AFRAID...*

ENOUGH! ONE LAST TIME WILL I PROVE MYSELF TO YOU...AND NEVER AGAIN.

YOU ARE NOT THE ONLY ONE WHO IS WILLING TO DO WHAT MUST BE DONE.

IN TWO DAYS, MEET *OUR* CHALLENGE...

...AND WE WIL[L] ALL SEE WHA[T] MUST BE DONE.

ANY NEWS FROM DIANA? THE MEN ARE STARTING TO GET RESTLESS.

NOTHING YET--

*--BUT SHE PROMISED SHE'D FIX THIS CONFLICT WITH OUR SISTERS IN THEMYSCIRA.

*THAT THIS ISLAND COULD BE *OUR* HOME, TOO...

*WE JUST NEED TO GIVE HER A LITTLE MORE *TIME*."

THAT DOESN'T EXCUSE WHAT YOU HAVE DONE.

YOU ARE MISTAKEN IF YOU THINK WE WILL NOW SIT BACK AND WATCH OUR PEOPLE DIE. WE WILL DO **WHATEVER** IS NECESSARY.

YOUR STERILE PLANET PALES IN COMPARISON TO THE GLORY OF GAEA.

SO MUCH HAS CHANGED SINCE YOU CRASH-LANDED.

YOU ARE NOT THE ONLY ONE HERE FROM ANOTHER PLANET.

WHAT IF YOU **COULD** GO HOME AGAIN?

WE ARE LISTENING.

THERE IS NOTHING WE WANT MORE.

BUT, THIS CAVERN IS ALL THAT IS LEFT OF OUR SHIP.

WHAT IF IT **WASN'T** NECESSARY? WHAT IF YOU COULD GO HOME AGAIN? WOULD YOU EVEN WANT TO?

CYBORG, IS IT POSSIBLE?

IT'S WORTH A TRY, BUT I'LL NEED TO RUN A FEW SCANS OF THE SHIP FIRST TO KNOW FOR SURE.

THE ESSENTIAL COMPONENTS LIKE THE COMPUTERS AND NAVIGATION SYSTEM ARE ALL STILL INTACT...

...AND THE REACTOR CORE IS NOT DISSIMILAR FROM OTHER ALIEN TECH WE'VE ENCOUNTERED.

IT WILL TAKE SOME TIME-- BUT IT *CAN* BE DONE.

WELL?

WE DID NOT DARE TO HOPE THAT IT COULD BE POSSIBLE... TO GO HOME AGAIN.

THANK YOU.

OUR SISTERS MAY NOT HAVE WANTED TO SHARE *PARADISE ISLAND* WITH THE MEN, BUT THERE IS A REASON YOUR MOTHER ARRANGED TO TRADE OUR SONS TO HEPHAESTUS.

WE ARE WARRIORS...

...NOT MURDERERS.

NOT EVERYONE, DESSA.

BUT THOSE WITH BLOOD ON THEIR HANDS...

...THEY WILL BE BROUGHT TO JUSTICE.

AMAZONS! WHAT HAVE YOU DONE?!

WE DID WHAT WAS NECESSARY TO *FINALLY* CLEANSE THIS ISLAND OF THE VERMIN YOU WOULD HAVE ALLOWED TO OVERRUN US.

THEY WERE OUR BROTHERS...

...THEY WERE DEFENSELESS...

...AND YOU SLAUGHTERED THEM IN COLD BLOOD.

THEY WERE PARASITES...

...AND LIKE YOU ARE ABOUT TO...THEY GOT WHAT THEY DESERVED: *DEATH.*

FOR MY HATRED *IS* LIKE A FIRE...

NNGH!

...AND YOU...

MMF!

...THE FUEL FOR MY RAGE!

YOUR RAGE BLINDS YOU!

YOU CALL YOURSELF THE *PERFECT* AMAZON.

BUT FROM EVERYTHING I HAVE SEEN SO FAR...

...YOU HAVE ONLY SHOWN YOURSELF TO BE A *COWARD*...

...A COWARD... AND A *BULLY*.

YOU STAND THERE AND THROW WORDS RATHER THAN PUNCHES!

IT'S *YOU* WHO IS THE COWARD!

YOU HAVE NO IDEA WHAT IT MEANS TO BE A WARRIOR OF THEMYSCIRA.

AN AMAZON KNOWS WHAT IT MEANS TO MAKE MISTAKES... BECAUSE THAT IS HOW SHE LEARNS.

NNG!

I WISH I COULD GO BACK AND CHANGE THE EVENTS THAT BROUGHT US HERE.

BUT OUR BROTHERS ARE *STILL* DEAD.

AND YOU WILL STILL HAVE TO ATONE FOR YOUR PART IN THAT.

NO! IT'S NOT POSSIBLE! DAMN YOU, GIRL!

THOSE OF YOU WHO PARTICIPATED IN THE RAID ON THE MEN'S VILLAGE WILL BE BROUGHT TO JUSTICE.

WE HAVE FORGOTTEN **WHO** AND **WHAT** WE ARE.

AN AMAZON OF THEMYSCIRA IS MORE THAN JUST A WARRIOR.

SHE IS A SISTER...

...A MOTHER...

...A LOVER...

...A FRIEND.

SHE DOES NOT RUN FROM HER FEARS...

...SHE EMBRACES THEM...

...BECAUSE SHE KNOWS THAT TRUE STRENGTH IS THAT OF CHARACTER.

...YOU WILL BETRAY US ALL...JUST AS YOUR MOTHER DID ME.

YOU CAN'T HELP YOURSELF.

THE SAME WEAKNESS FLOWS THROUGH YOUR VEINS...

THHUNK

NOOOO!!!

WE GAVE OUR OTHERS A PROPER AMAZON FUNERAL. AND IT WAS AGREED THAT NEVER AGAIN WOULD ANOTHER MALE CHILD BE FORCED FROM HIS FAMILY AND HIS HOME.

THOSE WHO PARTICIPATED IN THE RAID WERE SENT TO HEPHAESTUS TO SERVE AND ATONE IN HIS SMELTER, LIKE THEIR BROTHERS BEFORE THEM.

AND DONNA? SHE WAS BANISHED FROM PARADISE ISLAND FOREVER FOR HER CRIMES, AND TAKEN TO A PRISON ON MOUNT OLYMPUS.

I DON'T THINK WE'LL EVER KNOW WHAT DROVE DERINOE TO DO WHAT SHE DID. BUT SHE TAUGHT ME A VALUABLE LESSON.

BEING QUEEN IS ABOUT BALANCE AND RESPECT. CHANGE IS INEVITABLE. WE CAN'T CONTINUE AS WE ARE. BUT WE NEEDN'T TEAR OURSELVES APART BEFORE WE EVEN BEGIN TO TRY.

VERY DAY I AM MINDED OF WHAT I HAVE LOST.

AN OLD CRONE, ON AN ISLAND OF WOMEN WHO NEVER AGE.

WASTED! MY YOUTH...MY STRENGTH...MY BEAUTY...

...SACRIFICE...REPAID WITH ARROGANCE... AND BETRAYAL.

SUCH IS MY STORY.

QUEEN ALCIPPE. YOU GROW *MORE* BEAUTIFUL WITH EACH PASSING YEAR.

TRULY THE AMAZONS HAVE DISCOVERED THE FOUNTAIN OF YOUTH.

DO NOT WASTE MY TIME WITH FALSE FLATTERY, AMBASSADOR CHARAX. WHY ARE YOU HERE?

A WITCH, BY THE NAME OF HECATE, SKILLED IN THE ART OF NECROMANCY, IS RAISING AN ARMY OF THE UNDEAD ON THE ISLAND OF CRETE.

KING KLEOMENES THOUGHT IT ONLY RIGHT TO WARN YOU.

SO HE MIGHT HAVE SAID...

BUT YOU ARE HERE ON A *FOOL'S* ERRAND, CHARAX.

THERE IS NO ARMY ON EARTH STRONG ENOUGH TO THREATEN PARADISE ISLAND.

YOUR MAJESTY. FORGIVE US IF WE HAVE OVERSTEPPED. IT IS *ONLY* THAT KING KLEOMENES PLACES GREAT VALUE ON THE DEVELOPING RELATIONSHIP BETWEEN OUR TWO PEOPLES.

SO WE ARE AGREED.

THE MESSENIANS WILL NOT COME TO THE AID OF THEIR SPARTAN NEIGHBORS, AND THE GREEKS IN ATHENS WILL ONLY LEARN OF THIS BATTLE FROM THE SONGS SUNG OF OUR RETRIBUTION.

RALLY THE TROOPS. WE ATTACK AT DAYBREAK.

THE AMAZONS PACKED UP AND LEFT THE SPARTAN SHORES THAT SAME NIGHT.

FROM THAT DAY FORWARD, NO MAN WAS ALLOWED TO STEP FOOT ON OUR ISLAND.

WE HAD BEEN BETRAYED BY THE COWARDICE OF MEN, AND WE ONLY NEED LEARN THAT LESSON ONCE.

HECATE SOON GREW BORED TERRORIZING GREECE AND SPARTA AND MOVED NORTH TO NEW CONQUESTS.

AND ME?

I WAS AN OLD CRONE. NO LONGER WORTHY OF THE LOVE OF OUR STRONG AND BEAUTIFUL QUEEN.

I HID MYSELF AWAY AND WATCHED AS HIPPOLYTA GREW IN WISDOM AND MAJESTY THROUGH THE CENTURIES. AND I WATCHED...

...I WATCHED AS SHE, LIKE HER MOTHER BEFORE HER, ALLOWED HERSELF TO FALL VICTIM TO THE DECEPTION OF A MAN.

TONIGHT WE DINE IN THEMYSCIRA!

WONDER WOMAN

WONDER WOMAN ISSUE FORTY • MEREDITH FINCH WRITER • DAVID FINCH PENCILLER • JONATHAN GLAPION INKER • PETER STEIGERWALD COLORIST

ROB LEIGH LETTERER • BILL SIENKIEWICZ MOVIE POSTER VARIANT COVER • DAVID PIÑA ASSISTANT EDITOR • MATT IDELSON GROUP EDITOR • BOB HARRAS SENIOR VP — EDITOR IN CHIEF DC COMICS

RATED T TEEN   DAN DIDIO AND JIM LEE CO-PUBLISHERS • GEOFF JOHNS CHIEF CREATIVE OFFICER • DIANE NELSON PRESIDENT   DC COMICS

MAY 2015

"Clear storytelling at its best. It's an intriguing concept and easy to grasp."—THE NEW YORK TIMES

"Azzarello is rebuilding the mythology of Wonder Woman."—CRAVE ONLINE

START AT THE BEGINNING!

WONDER WOMAN VOLUME 1: BLOOD

WONDER WOMAN VOL. 2: GUTS

by BRIAN AZZARELLO and CLIFF CHIANG

WONDER WOMAN VOL. 3: IRON

by BRIAN AZZARELLO and CLIFF CHIANG

SUPERGIRL VOL. 1: LAST DAUGHTER OF KRYPTON

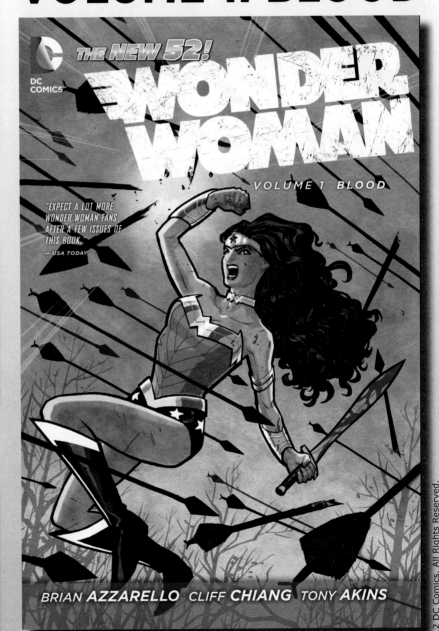

© 2012 DC Comics. All Rights Reserved.

DC COMICS™

"Writer Geoff Johns and artist Jim Lee toss you–and th
heroes–into the action from the very start and don't put
the brakes. DC's über-creative team craft an inviting world
those who are trying out a comic for the first time. Lee's ar
stunning."—USA TOD

"A fun ride."—I

START AT THE BEGINNING

JUSTICE LEAGUE
VOLUME 1: ORIGIN
GEOFF JOHNS and JIM LEE

**JUSTICE LEAGUE
VOL. 2: THE VILLAIN'S
JOURNEY**

**JUSTICE LEAGUE
VOL. 3: THRONE OF
ATLANTIS**

**JUSTICE LEAGUE
OF AMERICA VOL. 1:
WORLD'S MOST
DANGEROUS**